HE IS MY SHEPHERD

Scripture is from the *International Children's Bible*, New Century Version © 1986 by Sweet Publishing.

HE IS MY SHEPHERD
© 1989 by Multnomah

Printed in Mexico

Library of Congress Cataloging-in-Publication Data

Haidle, David.
    He is my shepherd / David and Helen Haidle.
        p.   cm.
    Summary: Presents the text of the twenty-third psalm and elaborates on the meaning of each line.
    ISBN 0-88070-278-8
    1. Bible O.T. Psalms XXIII—Juvenile literature. [1. Bible. O.T. Psalms XXIII—Criticism, interpretation,
etc.] I. Haidle, Helen. II. Title.
BS1450 23d.H33 1989
223'.209505—dc20   89-31428
                                                                                        CIP
                                                                                        AC

96 97 98 - 10 9 8 7 6 5

Dedicated to our Good Shepherd,
who laid down his life for his sheep.

The Lord is my shepherd.
    I have everything I need.
He gives me rest in green pastures.
    He leads me to calm water.
    He gives me new strength
For the good of his name,
    he leads me on paths that are right.
Even if I walk
    through a very dark valley,
I will not be afraid
    because you are with me.
Your rod and your walking stick
    comfort me.

You prepare a meal for me
    in front of my enemies.
You pour oil on my head.
    You give me more than I can hold.
Surely your goodness and love will be with me
    all my life.
And I will live in the house of the Lord
    forever.

Psalm 23, International Children's Bible

The LORD is my shepherd;
    I shall not want.
He maketh me to lie down in green pastures;
    he leadeth me beside the still waters.
He restoreth my soul;
    he leadeth me in the paths of righteousness
    for his name's sake.
Yea, though I walk through the valley
    of the shadow of death,
    I will fear no evil;
    for thou art with me;
    thy rod and thy staff they comfort me.
Thou preparest a table before me
    in the presence of mine enemies;
    thou anointest my head with oil;
    my cup runneth over.
Surely goodness and mercy
    shall follow me all the days of my life;
    and I will dwell in the house of the LORD
    forever.

Psalm 23, King James Version

HE IS MY SHEPHERD

by
Helen Haidle
illustrated by
David Haidle

Psalm 23 is a poem that was written and sung by David, one of the greatest kings in the land of Israel. David lived about a thousand years before Christ was born. He was the youngest of eight brothers and was given the lowly task of caring for his father's flock of sheep on the hills surrounding the little town of Bethlehem. While David was a shepherd boy, he was chosen by the Lord and annointed to be king over the people of Israel.

In this poem, David puts himself in the place of the sheep, and he calls the Lord his "shepherd." David may have played a harp or lyre and sung this song while he tended his own flock.

As you read Psalm 23, you will be thrilled to see and understand that the Lord is *your* Shepherd, that he takes care of you just as faithfully as a shepherd takes care of his precious sheep.

The Lord Is My Shepherd

Look at *who* my shepherd is—the Lord, God Almighty, maker of heaven and earth and all that exists! When I look through a telescope, peer into a microscope, or study nature, I get a glimpse of the amazing universe he created.

Thank you, Lord, for who you are and for all you have made.

This Lord of the universe calls me by name and says I'm his precious lamb. He lovingly holds my life in his hand. Even though I can't see him, he is here with me and will never leave me.

Lord, I'm amazed that you know me so well. You even know the number of hairs on my head!

I Have Everything I Need

A bitter winter storm blows outside this cave, but the sheep are enjoying their loving shepherd's care. They belong to him, so they don't need to worry. If they have him, they have everything.

Lord, sometimes my worries and problems seem so big. But they aren't too big for you, and I know you will take care of me in tough times.

He Gives Me Rest In Green Pastures

When sheep finish grazing they lie down to chew their cud so the food will digest. Unless they feel safe, they can't relax and lie down in the pasture. Nothing makes them feel safer or quiets them more than the presence of their shepherd.

Lord, when I lie down to sleep tonight, help me relax and rest. You are as close to me as my breath.

He Leads Me To Calm Water

Sheep are timid and easily frightened. Rushing streams and noisy, bubbling springs of water scare them. When they are thirsty, they would rather drink from disease-filled mudholes. So the shepherd patiently searches for calm, quiet pools of fresh water where he can lead the sheep to drink in peace.

Lord, when I get scared and upset, lead me to a quiet time with you.

He Gives Me New Strength

When a sheep has a heavy coat of wool, it can fall upside down on its back like a turtle. The hot sun on the sheep's belly can bring death in a few hours if the sheep is unable to get up. The careful shepherd keeps track of his sheep. When one is missing, he immediately begins searching until he finds it.

The search is over, the shepherd rejoices! He gladly carries his lost lamb home. While the sheep regains its strength, it snuggles on the shepherd's strong shoulders.

Lord, I'm thankful that you're always ready to help me when I'm in a mess. I'm glad you're not mad at me. Thanks for your strength when I'm down.

For The Good Of His Name,
He Leads Me On Paths That Are Right

Sheep can be stubborn—they want to travel their own easy way rather than follow the shepherd's direction. But only he can choose the paths that lead to high mountain pastures, lush and green. The sheep will be glad they followed his leading.

Lord, you know I don't always want to do what I'm told. Help me choose to obey you and do what is right today.

Even If I Walk Through A Very Dark Valley I Will Not Be Afraid, Because You Are With Me

A dark valley is a scary place to be. Sheep do not want to walk through shadowy pathways and deep ravines, but they learn to overcome fear when the shepherd is by their side. They huddle close to him as he leads them through the valley.

Lord, you know everything that scares me. You even know the things I'm afraid might happen to me. I'm glad you're with me no matter what happens.

Your Rod And
Your Walking Stick Comfort Me

The rod is a heavy club that fits in the shepherd's hand. Hours of practice help the shepherd throw it with speed and accuracy. It's the main weapon used to defend the flock.

The shepherd uses his long, slender walking stick to show affection to his sheep. He rubs his staff gently against their sides or uses it to pull a shy lamb closer.

Lord, when I feel lonely, help me remember you want me to be close to you. Your love for me feels like a big warm hug!

You Prepare A Meal For Me In Front Of My Enemies

Danger is everywhere . . . under rocks, over the hill, and even in the grass. The watchful shepherd must search for and pull out poisonous flowering weeds that grow in the meadow. Even a nibble on them can paralyze and kill a lamb.

Defending a helpless flock requires constant alertness.
Only the shepherd's quick action can save the sheep
from attack so they can eat in safety and peace.

Lord, sometimes I've been in danger and didn't even know it. Thank you
for the times and many ways you've saved me from trouble.

You Pour Oil On My Head

In the summer, nasal flies torment a flock. These pests buzz around trying to lay their eggs on the sheep's wet nose. When the eggs hatch into worms, they burrow up the nose and cause terrible irritation. When the flies attack, a sheep frantically shakes its head and stamps its feet, unable to eat or rest as it tries to escape the tormentors. As the shepherd pours protective oil on its nose and head, the sheep immediately becomes calm and can begin to feed quietly again.

Lord, calm me down when I feel like everyone is picking on me. Help me forgive and love those who hurt and bother me.

You Give Me More Than I Can Hold

At the end of the day the shepherd examines each sheep for cuts, scratches, or fever. He speaks lovingly to them while they drink from an overflowing basin of cool water; he makes sure they have all they want to drink. He delights in caring for his sheep.

Thanks, Lord, for all your good gifts in my life! I love juicy strawberries, delicate snowflakes, sandy beaches, pets, sunshine, my family and friends. Thanks for giving me all these joys because you love me.

Surely Your Goodness And Love Will Be With Me All My Life

The shepherd's tender goodness has been steady—through the seasons of chilling winds and blazing sun, in hunger and thirst, in storms and dangers, during illness and the attack of enemies. His faithfulness has brought the sheep through discouragement, trouble, and weakness. They have learned that he is completely trustworthy.

In the same way, the Lord can be trusted in the seasons and storms of my life. He has made very good plans for me, and he holds me close in his love.

Lord, I know that you won't leave me or quit loving me, even when it seems that others do. I'm glad you don't ever give up on me. Help me to confidently trust you all the days of my life.

And I Will Live In The House Of The Lord Forever

Just as the shepherd knows each of his lambs by name and can tell them apart, so the Lord knows all about me and loves me. He even knows the day of my death, when I will go to live with him forever.

What a special Forever that will be. A new heaven and a new earth where the lion and lamb lie down in peace. No more tears or pain.

My loving Shepherd will take me to his special home, and that will be something greater than I could ever imagine!

Lord, I know it will be more fun than making a snow fort or building a treehouse . . . always day and never night . . . no flu or colds . . . no bedtime, no sadness, no worries or fears . . . no more goodbyes or death . . . and I will see you face to face. I want to sit on your lap and hug you.
YOU ARE MY GOOD SHEPHERD.